On Midland Lines

Derek Huntriss

First published 1992

ISBN 0 7110 2090 6

© Ian Allan Ltd 1992

Published by Ian Allan Ltd, Shepperton, Surrey; and
printed by Ian Allan Printing Ltd at their works at
Coombelands in Runnymede, England.

Front cover:
*Former Midland Railway '3F' 0-6-0 No 43832
heads south through Burton-on-Trent with a
coke train on 12 April 1958.*

This page:
*On the former Midland route from Manchester
to Derby, Stanier '8F' 2-8-0 No 48442 climbs
through Buxworth cutting with a freight from
Gowhole Yard to Buxton on 3 February 1968.
This section of the route near Chinley was
widened to accommodate four tracks in 1902
and the tunnel which had existed at Buxworth
was demolished to be replaced by a deep
cutting. D. Huntriss*

Introduction

Absorbed into the London, Midland & Scottish Railway in early 1923, the Midland Railway was one of those companies which had put its unmistakable stamp on so much that it owned, that even in the 1950s and 1960s there were still many signs in evidence.

For the first time in colour, this title portrays many of the former Midland Railway routes as they were seen by the dedicated photographers who have generously provided the material which makes up the contents of this book.

Set out geographically in three basic sections, the title follows the routes from London St Pancras to Derby, Bristol-Derby and Derby-Carlisle via Sheffield, Leeds, Bradford and Skipton.

Centred at Derby, the Midland Railway had developed a small engine policy. Despite supplying the Somerset & Dorset Joint Railway with '7F' 2-8-0s, the Midland used their well tried and tested range of 0-6-0s for freight workings with nothing larger than 4-4-0s for passenger duties.

Following the formation of the LMS, there was a period of slow consolidation and it took six or seven years before the old distinctive MR livery had totally disappeared. Such was the influence of Derby after the Grouping that the mass production of Class 4F 0-6-0s continued until the voices of the various operating departments were eventually heard. Following the introduction of the ill-designed LMS Beyer-Garratt class by Fowler in 1927, a more organised response to motive power requirements began to emerge. For express and mixed traffic duties, Stanier introduced the 'Jubilee' and Class 5 4-6-0s. The heterogeneous collection of small tank locomotives was gradually replaced by more standardised 2-6-2 and 2-6-4 tank locomotives and for heavy freight duties, Stanier introduced the Class 8F 2-8-0s. It was this mixture of motive power, and the new BR Standard classes, that was to be found on the former Midland routes in the 1950s and 1960s. Many examples of these classes are illustrated in this title and where appropriate, their activities after leaving former MR lines are described.

As we capture the unique character of the Midland routes in the final years of BR steam operation, we must offer thanks to all the photographers whose work appears in these pages. Without their efforts and care in preserving their irreplaceable images, this title would not have been possible.

Derek Huntriss
Camborne, Cornwall
June 1992

Right
Stanier LMS 0-4-4T No 41900 awaits departure from Upton-on-Severn with the branch train for Tewkesbury and Ashchurch on 19 July 1958. At that time Upton-on-Severn was the terminus of the truncated Midland branch to Great Malvern. *W. Potter*

Below:
A fine selection of ex-works locomotives is present in this early 1956 view of Derby MPD (17A). Occupying a large area to the east of the goods avoiding lines and adjoining the main lines towards Spondon, the depot also borders the locomotive works. Like most large Midland Railway sheds, Derby had, in addition to the usual depot facilities, a roundhouse for the stabling of locomotives. *J. M. Jarvis*

Left:
LMS 'Jubilee' 4-6-0 No 45620 North Borneo prepares to depart from St Pancras. Allocated to Nottingham (16A) for many years until transferred to Burton-on-Trent (17B) in November 1961, No 45620 saw most of its service on the Midland main line. J. M. Jarvis

Right
The preserved Midland 'Compound' 4-4-0 No 1000 departs from St Pancras piloting 'Royal Scot' 4-6-0 No 46106 Gordon Highlander with the 1.55pm St Pancras-Manchester on 27 April 1960. No 1000 had arrived in the capital from Derby on Easter Monday when it double-headed 'Jubilee' 4-6-0 No 45569 Tasmania with the 12.22pm Manchester-Derby train which had been extended to St Pancras for the holiday traffic. No 1000 was brought to London to work excursions from King's Cross to Doncaster during the holiday week. On the first trip, on 20 April, No 1000, which was manned by a Kentish Town crew, was assisted by Western Region 4-4-0 No 3440 City of Truro to Doncaster. Unfortunately, on the return journey, No 3440 succumbed to overheating and was detached at Fletton Junction, allowing No 1000 to make a spirited return unassisted. A. Turner

Left:
Designed by Fowler and introduced in 1930, this useful class of 70 2-6-2Ts was mainly used on local passenger and freight workings. No 40026, seen here awaiting its next turn of duty at St Pancras, was one of 19 members of the class to be fitted with condensing apparatus in an attempt to reduce exhaust emissions in long tunnel sections such as the London Metropolitan 'widened lines'. The class was an early victim of modernisation following the introduction of diesel multiple-units and the first withdrawals occurred during 1959 almost halving the numbers of this class. No 40026 remained active, working from Kentish Town, until November 1962 before being removed to Derby Works where it was broken up in March 1963.
Colour Rail

Right:
LMS rebuilt 'Patriot' 4-6-0 No 45531 Sir Frederick Harrison, then allocated to Liverpool Edge Hill (8A), has arrived in London with an excursion on 28 June 1963 and is depicted at Cricklewood (14A) MPD. The rebuilt members of this class were fitted with taper boilers, double chimneys, modern smoke deflectors and worked expresses and fitted freights until their final withdrawal. No 45531 became one of the last three active members of the class allocated to Carlisle Kingmoor (12A) and was not withdrawn until November 1965. Colour-Rail

Left:
A typical Sunday view of Kentish Town (14B) MPD, taken on 3 March 1957, depicts a wide assortment of Midland line motive power which includes '4Fs', 'Jubilees', a 2-6-4 tank and a BR Standard Class 5 4-6-0. T. B. Owen

Far left:
This fine action shot depicts LMS 'Jubilee' 4-6-0 No 45641 Sandwich working an up Manchester express near Elstree on Saturday 28 February 1959. Allocated to Nottingham (16A) MPD from October 1957 until December 1961 when it was transferred to Burton-on-Trent (17B) MPD, No 45641 remained a Midland line engine for much of its working life. Final withdrawal for No 45641 came in September 1964, a year which saw 66 members of the class removed from traffic. T. B. Owen

Left:
Taken only 40min after the previous picture, this view portrays LMS Class 4 2-6-4T No 42156 with an up slow working. Designed by Fairburn and introduced in 1945, this class was one of the few types of locomotive to be allocated to all the regions of British Railways and during the years from 1957 to 1967 there were frequent interchanges of these locomotives between the individual regions. A Kentish Town (14B) locomotive for much of its working life, No 42156 ended her days working from Birkenhead (9H) MPD after brief allocation to Rowsley (17C) and Derby (16C) MPDs. T. B. Owen

Right:
LMS Garratt 2-6-0+0-6-2 No 47982 works a Toton-Brent coal train north of Harpenden in October 1953. The LMS Garratt was a hybrid version of the highly successful Beyer Peacock design which was already carving a distinguished reputation as a locomotive of considerable ability. The LMS Garratt's operational problems were largely due to the Midland influence at Derby. The fitting of Class 4F axleboxes with typical Midland spring gear and Midland-type valve gear with poor cylinders and valves was enough to wreck a well-proven design.
J. M. Jarvis

Below right:
This fine evening study depicts LMS 2-6-2T No 40027 working a northbound suburban service south of Harpenden in 1955. One of the 19 locomotives in the class to be fitted with condensing apparatus, No 40027 was an early victim of modernisation, being withdrawn from Kentish Town (14B) MPD in November 1959. Stored at Cricklewood (14A) MPD until May 1960, it was despatched to Stratford Works and broken up during the same month. J. M. Jarvis

Far right:
One of the last working LMS '2P' 4-4-0s, No 40646, is seen at Bedford on 14 April 1962. It was working a special train organised by the Stephenson Locomotive Society which toured no fewer than seven branch lines during the course of the day. These fine looking 4-4-0s were of similar design to the 40332-40559 series and for many years were used on expresses. Latterly, they were confined to local passenger, freight and pilot duties. No 40646 was one of only 15 members of the class to survive into 1962; No 40670 of Dumfries (68B) being the last of the class to be withdrawn in December of that year.
Colour-Rail

Far left:
LMS Class 5 4-6-0 No 44667
hammers up the 1 in 119
grade to Sharnbrook summit
with a St Pancras-Derby
semi-fast on 30 August 1958.
One of 14 examples of that
class to be allocated to Derby
(17A) MPD at that time,
No 44667 remained a
Midland line locomotive until
it was reallocated from
Leicester Midland (15C) MPD
to Woodford Halse (2F) MPD
in October 1962. After a stay
of only three months, from
August to November 1963, at
Leicester Central (15E) MPD,
No 44667 saw out the rest of
her days in the northwest of
England at Lancaster Green
Ayre (10J) and Carnforth
(10A) MPDs surviving at the
latter depot until withdrawal
in August 1967. T. B. Owen

Left:
Some 90min earlier at the
same location, BR Standard
Class 4 4-6-0 No 75063 coasts
down from Sharnbrook
summit with steam to spare
as it passes with an up local.
This type of locomotive,
slightly less powerful than
the BR Standard Class 5
4-6-0, was employed on all
but the heaviest trains.
Unlike the BR Standard Class
5 4-6-0s, several members of
the class were seemingly
picked at random to be fitted
with double chimneys, but it
appears that all of the
Southern Region-based
locomotives were eventually
converted. T. B. Owen

Right:
LMS '8F' 2-8-0 No 48490 approaches Sharnbrook summit with a down loaded mineral train on 18 September 1961. For many years Midland and LMS 0-6-0s were the mainstay of most Midland line freight services, but by this time much of the remaining coal, limestone and general traffic was handled by Stanier '8F' 2-8-0s and BR Standard '9F' 2-10-0s. A Toton (18A) based engine for much of its working life, No 48490 was allocated to Nottingham (16A) MPD when this picture was taken. Eventually, No 48490 was to complete her career in the northwest of England, being allocated to Northwich (9G) and Heaton Mersey (9F) MPDs before withdrawal from the latter depot in September 1965. *M. Mensing*

Far right:
A Bristol Barrow Road (82E) locomotive for much of its working life, LMS 'Jubilee' 4-6-0 No 45685 Barfleur hammers up the grade towards Sharnbrook summit with a down Bradford express on 30 August 1958. Always a Midland line engine, No 45685 remained at Bristol Barrow Road MPD until April 1964, when it was despatched to Birds' scrap yard at Risca where it was broken up in January 1965. *T. B. Owen*

Above:
Hauling a neat rake of plum and spilt-milk liveried BR Mk 1 stock, LMS 'Jubilee' 4-6-0 No 45641 Sandwich heads an up Bradford-St Pancras express near Kettering station on Saturday 28 August 1954. T. B. Owen

Left:
LMS Garratt 2-6-0+0-6-2 No 47996 heads north through Kettering, also on 28 August 1954. The revolving 10-ton capacity coal bunker is clearly visible. Powered by a small reversible two-cylinder steam engine, the bunker could be oscillated. If the machinery was in decent order, three or four full revolutions, taking about 90sec were usually enough to trim all remaining coal in the bunker down to the shovel plate.
Colour-Rail/T. B. Owen

Above:
Heading a rake of mainly wooden-bodied coal wagons, LMS '8F' 2-8-0 No 48470 heads an up freight near Kettering, also on 28 August 1954. The splendid array of Midland semaphores make a splendid picture. It is interesting to note that in 1895 the Midland Railway had 12,796 signals in operation which meant an average of 9.7 signals for every mile of track. The distinctive appearance of Midland apparatus was entirely *due to the fact that the equipment had always been produced by the company itself from a very early stage. T. B. Owen*

Above:
This Sunday view of Market Harborough (15F) MPD taken on 23 August 1959 gives a good indication of the types of motive power allocated at that time. At the beginning of the 1960 summer timetable, the banking of loaded coal trains between Market Harborough and Kelmarsh, on the Northampton line, was discontinued, train loads being reduced accordingly, following which the depot's ex-LNWR 0-8-0s Nos 49444/7 were transferred

from Market Harborough to Wigan. Loss of the 0-8-0s left Market Harborough with only one engine, Midland '4F' 0-6-0 No 43977 which was used as goods yard pilot at Welham. This locomotive was later transferred to Leicester Midland (15C) MPD whereupon Market Harborough became a sub-shed of Leicester Midland.
On 14 September 1884, a new station was opened at Market Harborough by the LNWR, the MR paying a contribution towards its upkeep.

This Georgian style Grade II listed building was the subject of an £84,000 restoration which was completed in June 1978. Some have described the building as having 'Queen Anne' style, reminiscent of the work of Norman Shaw, though the original architect is unknown.
T. B. Owen

Above:
This picture taken on the approach to Wigston Magna station depicts Ivatt Class 4 2-6-0 No 43042 with the 5.20pm Leicester (London Road)-Bedford stopping train. This Midland line 2-6-0 remained allocated to Kettering (15B) MPD until September 1962 when it was transferred to Heaton Mersey (9F) MPD where it remained until withdrawal in February 1966. These modern locomotives were easily distinguishable by their extremely high running plates above the driving wheels. *Whilst this made their maintenance considerably easier, their outward appearance became somewhat ugly, earning them the nickname 'Flying Pigs'. Some members of the class were fitted with double chimneys during the course of their lives in accordance with their original design specifications, but by the end of their lives the whole class ended up with the single chimney arrangement. Being Class 4 locomotives most of their work was confined to local passenger and freight working,* but occasionally they could be seen piloting more powerful locomotives on expresses.
M. Mensing

Left:
Another lifelong Bristol Barrow Road 'Jubilee' No 45685 Barfleur has just passed Coaley station with the up 'Devonian' on 7 July 1962. On summer Saturdays this working was one of 30 up and 29 down passenger trains to operate between Bristol and Gloucester. M. Mensing

Right:
Stanier Class 5 4-6-0 No 45050 works the 11.20am Newquay-Wolverhampton past the closed station at Charfield on 31 July 1965. This diagram was routed via Stratford-on-Avon to Wolverhampton Low Level. Careful observation will detect a large lump of coal dropping from the well-filled tender. Scene of the well-documented disaster in October 1928, it is interesting to note that the signal box, visible at the other end of the station, became redundant as part of the Bristol MAS scheme and was dismantled by Dean Forest Railway Society volunteers in November 1971 for re-erection at their site at Parkend. M. Mensing

Left:
LMS '4F' 0-6-0 No 44045 arrives at Dudbridge Junction with a freight from Stroud Wallbridge on 5 October 1962. At this point the trucks were deposited in a siding, the locomotive working the branch to Nailsworth on the right of the picture. On return from Nailsworth the freight would be combined for the return run to Gloucester via Stonehouse. *W. Potter*

Right:
On 12 May 1965, BR Standard Class 2 2-6-0 No 78004 is working a goods train from Nailsworth to Gloucester and has stopped at Stonehouse Wharf to allow the fireman to open the crossing gates. After drawing the freight forward past the gates, the guard would descend from his brake van in order to close the gates behind the train. Only seven months after this picture was taken No 78004 was withdrawn from traffic at Gloucester Horton Road (85B) MPD. It was then despatched to Birds' yard at Morriston, Swansea, for breaking up. *W. Potter*

Far left:
Deeley Midland 0-4-0T No 41535 is about to cross Llanthony Road, Gloucester, en route from the main basin in Gloucester docks to High Orchard sidings in Gloucester on 4 June 1962. Of the eight members of this class surviving at that time, two were allocated to Gloucester Barnwood (85C) MPD for work in the docks, two were allocated to Burton-on-Trent (17B) MPD for use in the brewery sidings complex and the remainder were allocated to Staveley Barrow Hill (41E) MPD and were employed to work the Staveley Ironworks. At that time traffic in the docks included grain for milling, agricultural products, general cargo and timber which arrived by the canal and was despatched by rail. 1975 saw the closure of the former MR lines in Gloucester; the dock rail system passing into history. Today, the docks are being redeveloped for leisure pursuits, the route of the former MR branch from California Crossing to Southgate Street Crossing is now occupied by Gloucester's inner ring road. W. Potter

Left:
LMS 'Jubilee' 4-6-0 No 45605 Cyprus leaves Gloucester Eastgate and passes under the unique Barton Street Junction signalbox with a Bristol bound express in July 1963. Generally speaking, the Midland was a line with small neat signalboxes, made throughout of wood and painted yellow. The average Midland box had quite a short lever frame, partly because facing points and facing point locks were worked by the same lever and partly because the Midland was relatively sparing in the provision of shunting signals. Indeed, the largest Midland Railway box, at St Pancras Junction, had only 132 levers. The box floors were generally covered in linoleum and the lighting at night kept dim, the idea being to help the signalman to see the engine numbers by the aid of a large lamp fixed outside the box on the front. P. Riley

Above:
This timeless scene captured on 22 July 1961 shows Midland '3F' 0-6-0 No 43754 awaiting departure from Ashchurch with the branch train to Tewkesbury and Upton-on-Severn, the terminus of the truncated branch to Great Malvern. No 43754, one of the batch of 575 locomotives built by Johnson between 1888 and 1902 was approaching the end of its active life, Nos 43620, 43637 and 43669 being the only '3Fs' to survive into 1964. *W. Potter*

Right:
No apologies are made for the inclusion of this picture which captures the everyday scene on the Ashchurch-Upton-on-Severn branch over 30 years ago. Taken the day after the previous picture, Midland '3F' No 43754 is crossing the River Avon near Tewkesbury with a return working from Upton-on-Severn. *W. Potter*

Left:
Friday 11 April 1958 sees LMS '3F' 'Jinty' 0-6-0 No 47276 and WR 0-6-0PT No 8401 giving the 'Big Push' to a Bristol to York express up the Lickey incline through Bromsgrove station. T. B. Owen

Right:
LMS '4F' 0-6-0 No 44571 makes a cautious descent of the 1 in 37 gradient towards Bromsgrove with a loose-coupled freight on 20 October 1962. The normal procedure for downhill trains was to stop at Blackwell, whereupon the guard and Brakesman conferred. Then the signal to proceed was given and the train moved slowly downgrade whilst wagon brakes were applied. After this first part of the job, the fireman would look back to see that the guard had rejoined his brake van whereupon hand signals were exchanged. If appropriate, the fireman would apply the tender handbrake. Next, the driver would apply the engine brake and the object, after descending the bank, was to stop for water by Bromsgrove South signalbox. P. Riley

Above:
LMS Class 5 4-6-0 No 44944 heads a rake of mineral wagons up the 1 in 37 from Bromsgrove to Blackwell. Opened on 17 September 1840, the Birmingham and Gloucester included a two-mile incline at 1 in 37 from Bromsgrove to Blackwell. Climbing from the uplands of the Severn basin, the Lickey incline lifts the Birmingham-Bristol main line to the edge of the West Midlands plateau. For many years banking duties were performed by Class 3F 'Jinties' until 1919 when Derby Works stepped in with the four-cylinder 0-10-0 'Big Bertha' which performed admirably until withdrawn in 1956. The moving of BR's Western Region boundary north to Barnt Green in the late 1950s brought some Westernisation. A '52xx' 2-8-0T was the banker for some time, but the most suited for the job were the GW-designed '94xx' 0-6-0PTs. Steam survived on the Lickey until dieselisation brought the first Class 37 to the line. This arrived in the form of D6938 on 5 July 1964, when it was used for crew training. Colour-Rail

Above:
Midland '2P' 4-4-0 No 40486 passes Halesowen
Junction with the 4.35pm stopper from
Birmingham to Gloucester in May 1956. An early
victim of modernisation, No 40486 was
withdrawn from Bristol Barrow Road (22A) in
February 1957, being despatched to Derby
Works and broken up during the same month.
T. J. Edgington/Colour-Rail

Left:
On 29 July 1963, 'Derby 4' 0-6-0 No 44605 assists a
down coal train up the 1 in 85 gradient past
St Andrew's Junction, Birmingham. Adjacent to
Birmingham City's St. Andrew's football ground,
the roar of the crowd on Saturday afternoons
could be heard at this location. M. Mensing

Left:
Stranger on Midland lines, Sheffield Darnall
(41A) based Thompson 'B1' 4-6-0 No 61315 passes
through the disused platforms at Five Ways,
Birmingham, in July 1962. P. Riley

Above:
LMS 'Jubilee' 4-6-0 No 45682 Trafalgar awaits
departure from Platform 9 at Birmingham New
Street whilst working the 12.48pm York-Bristol
Temple Meads on 16 April 1960. The old station
at Birmingham New Street, built in 1854 and

extended in the 1880s, completely disappeared
during the rebuilding in the mid-1960s, the
entire track layout between the tunnels at the
east and west ends being remodelled.
M. Mensing

Far left:
Saltley (21A) based Ivatt Class 4 2-6-0 No 43036 draws away from Birmingham New Street, Platform 7, with empty stock on 7 July 1962. No 43036 had arrived in the Midland division platform with the 8.15am from Worcester Shrub Hill. New Street was unique, at this time, in Britain in that it was an open station without ticket barriers; this arrangement was the rule in the last century, but for many years all other major stations had been closed. The reason for the survival of this arrangement was that the main overbridge at New Street was also a public right of way — a facility which had to be incorporated in the new layout. M. Mensing

Above left:
This rare colour view shows the unique Midland Railway 0-10-0 No 58100, the famous Lickey Banker, in ex-works lined black livery outside Derby (17A) MPD in 1951. Making its first public appearance on New Year's Day 1920, the four-cylinder 0-10-0 No 2290 was specifically designed to assist trains up the Lickey incline, a task it must have performed at least 200,000 times over a period of 36 years before travelling back to its birthplace in the late afternoon of Monday 7 May 1956 to be broken up. E. Oldham/Colour-Rail

Below left:
Another rare colour picture, this time featuring the diminutive Johnson 0-4-0 inside cylinder tank No 41523 outside Derby MPD in March 1955. Introduced in 1897, this locomotive weighed only 32 tons and was allocated to Burton-on-Trent (17B) MPD for use in the brewery sidings complex. J. Davenport/Colour-Rail

Above:
This delightful study of ex-works LMS '3F' 0-6-0T 'Jinty' No 47377 was taken outside Derby MPD in November 1959. Introduced by the LMS in 1924, this ubiquitous class of shunting locomotives was based on a Johnson design of 1899 with detail alterations. With 415 examples built for the LMS *and seven for the Somerset & Dorset Joint Railway Company (taken into LMS stock in 1929) they were very common. Two LMS engines (Nos 7456 and 7533) were regauged to 5ft 3in and sent to the Northern Counties Committee section of the LMS in Ireland as NCC Nos 18 and 19. P. J. Hughes*

Below:
A locomotive type rarely photographed in colour, Johnson Midland 0-6-0 No 58175, stands outside Nottingham (16A) MPD in November 1959, evidence of its LMS ownership showing through the flaking paint on the tender. This class of engine, introduced in 1917, was the Johnson 5ft 3in design rebuilt with Belpaire firebox. P. J. Hughes

Above:
Displaced from LM West Coast main line duties, 'Royal Scot' 4-6-0 No 46157 The Royal Artilleryman was reallocated from Crewe North (5A) to Nottingham (16A) in November 1959, where it is seen shortly after arrival. Staying at

Nottingham until June 1961, No 46157 spent one year at Saltley (21A) and Carlisle Upperby (12B) MPDs before being allocated to Carlisle Kingmoor (12A) MPD where it survived until withdrawal in January 1964. P. J. Hughes

Right:
This line-up of condemned '4Fs' awaiting scrapping outside Nottingham MPD in November 1959 show a distinct Midland parentage. The line-up includes locomotive Nos 44018, 44555, 44021 and 44204. P. J. Hughes

This Derby designed class of 65 locomotives, introduced in 1953 replaced some of the ageing machinery still to be found on many regions of BR in the 1950s. Popular and versatile, these Standard Class 2 2-6-0s were ideal for branch line and secondary route workings such as trip freights and station pilot duties. Here, No 78020 is depicted outside Nottingham MPD in November 1959. After allocations to Annesley (16D), Springs Branch, Wigan (8F), Derby (16C) and Wellingborough (15A) MPDs, No 78020 arrived back at Nottingham in July 1966. No 78020 was one of only 12 members of the class to survive into 1967, their allocations being divided between Bolton (9K) and Lostock Hall (10D) MPD's. P. J. Hughes

Above:
The Cromford & High Peak Railway, or the Manchester, Buxton, Matlock & Midland Junction Railway, as it was later known, became vested in the Midland Railway in 1871. Early traffic carried was mainly limestone from the many quarries in the area although the line had been used for carrying coal, bricks, bone-manure and water. Opened throughout from Cromford to Whaley

Bridge in 1831, the C & HPR linked the termini of the Peak Forest Canal and the Cromford Canal crossing typically bleak Derbyshire moorland between these two waterways.

For a period in the mid-19th century passengers had been permitted to use the line in what was called a 'fly', a brake van with seats. This practice was discontinued after a fatal accident involving a passenger in 1877.

April 1967 marked the closure of much of the C & HPR and during the month a number of society specials, consisting mainly of brake vans and open wagons, had been hauled by a pair of 'J94' 0-6-0Ts over parts of the route.

Here, 'J94s' Nos 68006 and 68012 attack the 1 in 14 grade of Hopton Incline with the final ecs working on 30 April 1967.
D. Huntriss

Left:
Traversing the formidable barrier of the Peak, the Derby-Manchester route was boldly conceived and heavily engineered. One of the country's most scenic railway routes, its magnificent vistas rivalled some better known examples, such as those of the Settle & Carlisle line or the Callander & Oban. Here, the last active 'Britannia' Pacific No 70013 Oliver Cromwell is seen on 9 June 1968 emerging from Cressbrook tunnel (471yd) before the line enters Litton tunnel (515yd). Along this quarter of a mile, the passenger could catch a magnificent glimpse of the River Wye running in a deep, rocky, horseshoe shaped gorge. This special train, which returned to Nottingham via the Hope Valley route, was believed to be the last steam hauled passenger train to traverse the MR route through the Peak before closure.
P. J. Fitton

Right:
This magnificent view taken on 28 February 1968 shows LMS Class 8F 2-8-0 No 48532 with a rake of ballast wagons heading for Great Rocks past Buxton Junction. P. J. Fitton

Far left:
The snowy conditions of 3 February 1968 provided the potential for some unusual photographic opportunities. Here, LMS '8F' 2-8-0 No 48442 is seen through the arches of Chinley viaduct as it works a Gowhole Yard to Buxton freight. D. Huntriss

Left:
Moments later, No 48442 is seen drawing forward past Chinley South Junction box before reversing and crossing over to the down line. At the end of January 1968, single line working had been introduced between Chinley South Junction and Peak Forest as a result of engineering work in Dove Holes Tunnel. Steam working southeast of the area between Manchester and Buxton finally came to an end with the closure of Northwich (8E), Trafford Park (9E) and Buxton (9L) motive power depots from 4 March 1968, when the surviving steam-hauled freight workings were handed over to diesel traction. D. Huntriss

Above:
Almost eight years earlier, in July 1960, Stanier '8F' 2-8-0 No 48178 works a mixed freight between Chinley South Junction and Chapel-en-le-Frith. Being one of the most successful 2-8-0 designs, the LMS '8Fs' were used as a standard, being built for other companies during World War 2 until the evolution of the Riddles Austerity 2-8-0.

Rarely in the limelight, the Stanier 2-8-0s were almost always confined to freight and parcels duties, their main object in life being hard slog with heavy loads at relatively low speeds.
P. J. Hughes

Right:
For many years the mainstay of most Midland route freight services, the Midland and LMS 0-6-0s were gradually displaced by the LMS '8F' 2-8-0s and BR '9F' 2-10-0s. Here, LMS '4F' No 44101 pilots an unidentified Stanier 2-8-0 with a lengthy mineral train past the unmistakable array of signals at Chinley North Junction in July 1960. By late 1965 the ubiquitous Midland and LMS 0-6-0s had disappeared and the remaining steam-hauled Midland route coal, limestone and general traffic were handled by the '8F' and '9F' types until their displacement by diesel traction. P. J. Hughes

Left:
LMS '4P' 'Compound' 4-4-0 No 40907 heads a Manchester Central-Millers Dale working near Chapel-en-le-Frith on 30 April 1957. With the seat of LMS motive power provision still at Derby following the grouping of 1923, it was not surprising that the LMS increased the 45 compound 4-4-0s built in MR days with an additional 195 examples. Built between 1924 and 1927, these LMS examples had 6ft 9in diameter driving wheels, compared with the 7ft diameter of their MR predecessors. When this picture was taken only 89 examples were still in service, based at many depots on the BR system from Gloucester to Stranraer. Allocated to Sheffield Millhouses (19B), No 40907 remained operational from that depot until October 1960, when she was despatched to Doncaster Works for breaking up. The last survivor of the class was No 41168, which was withdrawn in July 1961. Colour-Rail

Right:
Stanier '8F' 2-8-0 No 48742 heads mineral empties from Northwich for Tunstead ICI sidings, south of Peak Forest Junction, past New Mills South Junction on 15 June 1957. The Disley cut-off continues straight out of the picture to the left and the line to New Mills and Marple bears off to the right. The Manchester line, in spite of its grading, was never regarded as a priority for Midland motive power, the Anglo-Scottish services always having first claim. In Midland days, 'Compound' 4-4-0s were first allocated to Trafford Park in 1909, and thereafter worked the principal expresses, but '700' class 4-4-0s were also in evidence along with Class 2 4-4-0s and Johnson 2-4-0s. By early LMS days, the picture had changed little; 'Compounds' Nos 1014-22 were at Trafford Park (and remained there until 1939), whilst Class 2s were used as pilots when occasion demanded. Colour-Rail

Left:
LMS 'Jinties' Nos 47629 and 47383 rest between duties at the NCB North Derbyshire Colliery at Williamthorpe in July 1967. Together with No 47289 they were the last three surviving members of this once numerous class. The large tank on the right of the picture, once used as a pit boiler, survived in the colliery yard as a water tank. Out-stationed from Westhouses (16G) and manned by NCB crews, the 'Jinties' were joined by a Class J94 Austerity 0-6-0ST from store at Buxton, but surprisingly this former Cromford and High Peak engine was not favoured by the NCB crews. By October 1967 steam was displaced with the introduction of diesel traction. *D. Huntriss*

Below:
BR-built 0-4-0ST No 47005 shunts the steelworks sidings at Staveley in clear winter sunlight on 21 December 1963. No 47005 was one of the second batch of five locomotives built at Horwich, the first five locomotives in this class being built to an original Kitson design and introduced in 1932 for use in brewery yards and other industrial complexes. *P. J. Hughes*

Left:
Midland '1F' 0-6-0T No 41835 poses for the camera at Staveley steelworks on 21 December 1963. This superheated tank engine was built as MR No 2003 in 1892, becoming MR No 1835 in 1907 and retained the same number when Grouped into the LMS in 1923. P. J. Hughes

Above:
Formerly allocated to Staveley Barrow Hill (41E), but usually housed on-site in the Staveley Ironworks two road sub-shed, Midland '1F' half-cab 0-6-0T No 41804 heads a mixed rake of wagons in the works on 21 December 1963. The survivors of this classic type of Midland shunter owed their longevity to a Midland Railway

agreement of 1866 which accepted responsibility for providing engines to shunt Staveley Ironworks for 100 years. Officially withdrawn in December 1966, No 41804 had been reported stored out of use at Barrow Hill and Canklow since the summer of 1965.
P. J. Hughes

Left:
Slogging through Dore & Totley up the 1 in 102 gradient to Bradway Tunnel, recently ex-works 'Jubilee' 4-6-0 No 45649 Hawkins heads a Newcastle-Bristol express in July 1960. Primarily allocated to sheds at Kentish Town, Derby, Bristol Barrow Road, Nottingham, Millhouses and Leeds Holbeck, the fleet of LMS 'Jubilees' was the staple motive power for Midland line expresses until the introduction of BR/Sulzer Type 4 'Peaks' in 1961. P. J. Hughes

Above:
LMS '4F' 0-6-0 No 44371 heads the 4.30pm Sheffield-Chinley local away from Dore & Totley station in September 1959. Whilst most of the Hope Valley local services ran to Chinley, certain trains worked through to Manchester Central via Romiley and Stockport Tiviot Dale. The only express service on this route was the 8.05am Sheffield Midland-Manchester which called at Hope, Chinley and Manchester Central. P. J. Hughes

Left:
One of the few remaining steam-hauled
passenger services to operate out of Sheffield
Midland in 1966 was the 9.39am to Chinley.
Pictured between Millhouses and Beauchief, this
diagram is being worked by Ivatt 2MT No 46465
in July 1966. Allocated to Buxton (9L), No 46465
was withdrawn in March 1967. P. J. Hughes

Above:
Allocated to Sheffield Grimsthorpe (41B),
Hughes Class 5MT 'Crab' No 42904 approaches
Beauchief station with a Manchester local in
July 1960. Many of this class were allocated to
depots in Lancashire and Yorkshire and before
the advent of the family car in the early 1960s,
they transported many thousands of
holidaymakers from the industrial centres of
these counties to seaside resorts mainly on the
west coast. After brief allocations to Canklow
(41D) and Stockport (9B), No 42904 was
transferred to Gorton (9G) in May 1963, where it
survived until withdrawn in May 1965.
P. J. Hughes

Above:
Stanier '8F' 2-8-0 No 48178 climbs the 1 in 100 gradient out of Sheffield through Beauchief station with an Engine Shed Sidings-Gowhole freight in July 1960. It was a fitting tribute to this fine class of locomotives that by the end of 1964 only 28 out of 666 examples had been taken out of service. However, time was not on the side of steam and in the next three and a half years, a massive total of 638 were condemned — such was the march of progress. P. J. Hughes

Below:
Allocated to Buxton in August 1961, Fowler Class 4MT No 42379 approaches Millhouses with the 9.39am Sheffield Midland-Chinley service on 3 April 1963. Reallocated to Newton Heath (26A) in July 1963, No 42379 survived at that depot until August 1964, after which it remained in store before despatch to the Central Wagon Co of Ince, Wigan, where it was broken up. One of four different designs of 2-6-4T introduced by the LMS, these classes were all handsome looking engines. In the main, their duties were secondary, but on occasions they could be called upon for express duties. P. J. Hughes

Left:
Depicted in October 1960, Stanier Class 5 4-6-0 No 44717 awaits its next turn of duty outside Sheffield Millhouses (41B) MPD. Despite increasing dieselisation, over half the class were still in service at the beginning of 1967. As their more illustrious counterparts were replaced by diesels, it fell to the 'Black 5s' to take over many expresses, either on regular diagrams or through diesel failures. No 44717 was one of the survivors, being allocated to Liverpool Edge Hill (8A) from July 1965, until its withdrawal in August 1967. P. J. Hughes

Above:
Returned to working order at Derby Works, MR No 1000 is seen at Sheffield Midland on its first revenue-earning outing on 30 August 1959, when it hauled a Stephenson Locomotive Society special from Birmingham, via Derby, to Doncaster and York and back. The veteran was reported to have attained 75mph near Stretton on the return journey. Allocated to Gloucester for many years No 41000 was withdrawn from Derby in October 1951. Initially stored for preservation at Derby, it was housed in the paint shop at Crewe Works before its return to Derby for restoration in March 1959. P. J. Hughes

61

Above:
The last surviving Midland-designed '4F' 0-6-0, No 43953, heads the 'Midland Locomotive Requiem' railtour past Staveley Barrow Hill on 16 October 1965. Prepared by the fitting staff (including the author's uncle) at Workington MPD, they were dismayed to learn that the locomotive was not to return after the railtour and was to be broken up at Crewe Works. At that time the '4F' was a far more reliable machine than the batch of Metrovick Co-Bos which had been allocated to Workington.
P. J. Hughes

Right:
Double chimney-fitted BR '9F' 2-10-0 No 92205 approaches Staveley Barrow Hill with an up fitted freight in November 1964.

Reallocated from Feltham (70B) to York (50A) only 12 months earlier, No 92205 remained at that depot until October 1966, when it was transferred to Wakefield (56A). Here it survived until it was withdrawn from traffic in June 1967.
P. J. Hughes

Above:
On the North Midland route between Tapton Junction and Rotherham, Stanier '8F' 2-8-0 No 48395 drifts down the 1 in 308 gradient from Staveley Barrow Hill with a down freight in November 1964. The most common item of freight over this route was coal which was mined in the many collieries which lay along the route from Leeds. P. J. Hughes

Top right:
Seen during a shed visit to Royston MPD on Sunday 19 July 1959, 'Jubilee' 4-6-0 No 45651 Shovell passes with a York-Bristol working. A Bristol Barrow Road (82E) locomotive, No 45651 and her crew had a taxing duty on this daily 212-mile turn. T. B. Owen

Bottom right:
This November 1963 view taken at Royston MPD depicts the usual Sunday line up of the depot's allocation of Stanier '8F' 2-8-0s. Their main weekday duties being the haulage of coal traffic over mineral or branch lines to the nearest sorting sidings. P. J. Hughes

Left:
This view, taken at 1.00am on a November morning in 1967, shows LMS 'Jubilee' 4-6-0 No 45562 Alberta at Normanton (55E) MPD. No 45562, kept in immaculate condition by members of the MNA enthusiast group, was booked to haul an enthusiasts' special later that day. During that year, eight surviving 'Jubilees' had soldiered on in the Leeds, Bradford and Wakefield areas, No 45562 being the last member of the class to be withdrawn.
D. Huntriss

Above:
Devoid of front numberplate and only weeks away from withdrawal, BR '9F' 2-10-0 No 92047 passes Normanton MPD with a Leeds Neville Hill-Stanlow empty oil tank working on 4 July 1967. This duty took the train via Goosehill Junction, Healey Mills and Standedge. For many years allocated to Bidston (6F) and used on the Birkenhead-Bidston ore traffic, No 92047 was reallocated to Birkenhead (8H) in February 1963 where it survived until it was withdrawn in September 1967. P. J. Fitton

Left:
LMS Class 5 4-6-0 No 45428 is portrayed outside Leeds Holbeck (55A) MPD in September 1963. Withdrawn from that depot in October 1967, No 45428 was fortunate to become one of 17 examples of the class which were to escape the cutters' torch. Now named Eric Treacy after the well-known Bishop and railway photographer, No 45428 is preserved on the North Yorkshire Moors Railway. Commonly known as 'Black 5s', the Stanier Class 5 4-6-0s were without doubt the most universally liked steam locomotives used by British Railways. Excepting parts of the Southern and Eastern regions, there was hardly a main line which was not graced by their presence. They could be usefully employed on anything from humble coal trains to all but the most crack express workings. *P. J. Hughes*

Right:
Patricroft (26F) based 'Jubilee' 4-6-0 No 45600 Bermuda awaits departure from the old Leeds City station with the 12.35pm to Manchester Exchange on Saturday 18 August 1962. At that time, the number of trains arriving at and leaving Leeds City totalled 500 and on a summer Saturday such as this, the number went up to almost 550. During the peak hours of 8am to 9am and 5pm to 6pm more than 80 trains arrived or departed. In a normal year 2¾ million passenger journeys commenced from Leeds and the number of parcels received or forwarded exceeded 2¾ million.
Development and planning of the remodelled layout for Leeds City was begun in 1959, the final redevelopment being formally declared operational on 17 May 1967, when the Lord Mayor of Leeds unveiled a commemorative plaque. *J. Duncan Gomersall*

Above:
Departing from Bradford Forster Square on
8 June 1967, LMS Class 5 4-6-0 No 44916 works
the 15.18 parcels train to Morecambe and
Heysham. Today's view at this location is
somewhat different in that new platforms have
been built and the sidings and signalbox have
now been removed. With the recent introduction
of electrically-hauled services between King's
Cross and Leeds, it is proposed that Bradford be
connected up in the not too distant future.
Allocated to Stockport (9B) MPD No 44916
survived at that depot for six months after this
picture was taken, being withdrawn in
December 1967. After spending one year in
store, it was despatched to Draper's yard in Hull
where it was broken up one month later.
P. J. Fitton

Right:
The late afternoon of 25 October 1966 sees much
activity at Skipton. LMS '3F' 0-6-0 'Jinty' No 47599
is busy shunting while Stanier '8F' 2-8-0 restarts
an eastbound freight and Ivatt Class 2 2-6-2T
No 41251 blows off impatiently on shed. For the
cameraman, Skipton was the base for
photography on the 8¼-mile branch to Spencer's
Lime Works at Grassington. Expanded in the
1960s, the traffic required up to three trains a
day to take out the loads. Closure of Skipton
(24G) MPD in April 1967 did not preclude former
Skipton-based Standard Class 4 4-6-0s from
continuing their duties on the Grassington
branch. A function which they carried on
virtually to the end of BR steam in August 1968.
Today, the Class 31 diesels rumble along the
branch to the Tilcon quarry at Swinden, taking

the early morning freight of lime hoppers down
into Leeds. P. J. Fitton

Above:
One of the last surviving 'Jubilee' 4-6-0s No 45593
Kolhapur blasts the last few yards up the
1 in 100 gradient to Giggleswick summit with the
3.18pm parcels from Bradford to Heysham in
March 1967. Withdrawn from traffic in October
1967, No 45593 was secured for preservation by
the Birmingham Railway Museum at Tyseley
and is currently operating in traffic on the Great
Central Railway at Loughborough. P. Riley

Right:
The desolation of the Settle & Carlisle route in
winter is captured in this picture of Stanier '8F'
2-8-0 No 48469 as it climbs towards Blea Moor in
April 1967. After the gruelling 14-mile climb of
1 in 100 from Settle Junction the crew could stop
at Blea Moor for water. Drivers of engines
wishing to do this would usually whistle, one
long and one short when passing through
Horton. This was not, of course, with the

intention of being heard at Blea Moor. The
message was telephoned ahead so if the
demands of traffic required it, the train could be
put into the loop. P. Riley

Above:
Stanier Class 5 climbs towards Blea Moor with an early morning freight in April 1967. When Blea Moor, exposed as it is, is not swept by driving rain, or lost in rolling mist, it can present an awe-inspiring sight. The line itself runs through squelching bogs on the flanks of Whernside which reaches the lofty altitude of 2,419ft. P. Riley

Right:
Another early morning view, this time taken in August 1966, sees LMS 'Jubilee' 4-6-0 No 45697 Achilles heading north over the towering arches of Ribblehead viaduct with a northbound freight.

Taking five years to construct, the 440yd 24-arch viaduct had every sixth arch strengthened and built to larger dimensions using the logic that if one arch should ever fall only five would follow.

After several years of campaigning against the threat of closure, the Settle & Carlisle is currently enjoying a reprieve, although the line over the viaduct has been singled and trains restricted to 30mph. R. Hobbs

Left:
Newton Heath (9D) based BR '9F' 2-10-0 No 92016 heads a down freight past the box at Dent on 14 July 1967. The station at Dent, at 1,145ft above sea level, was the highest on any English main line and was built as close as possible to the village of Dent, over four miles away. The station is reached by a crazy, corkscrew road which climbs 450ft in little more than half a mile. With a gradient of 1 in 5, it is commonly known as the Coal Road for it was originally built to serve coal pits, now long defunct, on Widdale Fell.

The '9F' was probably the most successful BR Standard type locomotive design and the last to be constructed, but sadly it was destined to be very shortlived. Many of this class had quite tragically short careers, being victims of the Modernisation Plan, and were still in excellent condition when withdrawn from service. In fact, during the course of 1965 the Western Region withdrew its entire allocation of the class which included some engines which had been built little more than five years earlier. *D. Huntriss*

Right:
The bright afternoon of 5 September 1960, sees Carlisle Kingmoor (12A) based '4F' 0-6-0 No 44181 heading an up goods away from Garsdale towards Rise Hill tunnel. Approximately half a mile south of Garsdale were situated the highest water troughs in Britain. Roughly half way between Leeds and Carlisle they were located several hundred feet above the valley floor at Garsdale where the line clings to the hillside.

Also close to Garsdale, the beerhead for visiting enthusiasts is the Moorcock Inn. If a visit to this hostelry happens to coincide with the local sheepdog trials, one can learn, amongst other things, the intricacies of sheep handling. *T. B. Owen*

Left:
Careful use of a 135mm telephoto lens emphasises the struggle of man and machine climbing towards Ais Gill summit.
With the snow covered slopes of Wild Boar Fell as a backdrop, Stanier Class 5 4-6-0 No 44912 struggles the last few yards up the 1 in 100 gradient to Ais Gill with an up freight in April 1967. P. Riley

Above:
Sunday 11 August 1968 marked the end of an era, with BR's last steam-hauled train running over standard gauge track. 420 passengers paid 15 guineas each for the 314-mile round trip from Liverpool to Carlisle, the price including a cold lunch, champagne and other refreshments, as well as a souvenir ticket and scroll.
The train was handled by four locomotives, the first being Stanier Class 5 No 45110, which stormed out of Liverpool Lime Street at the head of 10 coaches, departing simultaneously with

the 9.10am electric hauled express to Euston. 'Britannia' Pacific No 70013 Oliver Cromwell took over the train at Manchester Victoria for the journey to Carlisle via Blackburn, Hellifield and Ais Gill.
The return leg of this train was hauled by Stanier Class 5s Nos 44871 and 44781, seen here climbing along Mallerstang towards the crowds who had turned out at Ais Gill. D. Huntriss

Rear cover:
A regular Midland line performer, 'Britannia' Pacific No 70053 Moray Firth, heads the Glasgow-St Pancras 'Thames Clyde Express' through Dore & Totley in July 1960. P. J. Hughes

Above:
Midland no more. Situated on the secondary route from Barnt Green to Ashchurch, the derelict station at Ashton-under-Hill is depicted on 15 May 1973. Victim of the 'Beeching Plan', this secondary route closed to passenger traffic on 29 September 1962, the track being declared unfit for use.

With the advent of mass car ownership becoming more widespread in the early 1960s, it is hardly surprising that the growing road lobby forced many such routes to fall under the axe. W. Potter